Supply Contract

This contract should be used for local and international procurement
of high-value goods and related services including design

An NEC document

April 2013

Construction Clients' Board endorsement of NEC3

The Construction Clients' Board recommends that public sector organisations
use the NEC3 contracts when procuring construction. Standardising
use of this comprehensive suite of contracts should help to
deliver efficiencies across the public sector and promote behaviours
in line with the principles of *Achieving Excellence in Construction.*

Cabinet Office UK

NEC is a division of Thomas Telford Ltd, which is a wholly owned subsidiary of the Institution of Civil Engineers (ICE), the owner and developer of the NEC.

The NEC is a family of standard contracts, each of which has these characteristics:

- Its use stimulates good management of the relationship between the two parties to the contract and, hence, of the work included in the contract.
- It can be used in a wide variety of commercial situations, for a wide variety of types of work and in any location.
- It is a clear and simple document – using language and a structure which are straightforward and easily understood.

NEC3 Supply Contract is one of the NEC family and is consistent with all other NEC3 documents. Also available are the Supply Contract Guidance Notes and Flow Charts.

ISBN (complete box set) 978 0 7277 5867 5
ISBN (this document) 978 0 7277 5895 8
ISBN (Supply Contract Guidance Notes) 978 0 7277 5931 3
ISBN (Supply Contract Flow Charts) 978 0 7277 5933 7

First edition 2009
Reprinted 2010
Reprinted with amendments 2013

British Library Cataloguing in Publication Data for this publication is available from the British Library.

Typeset by Academic + Technical, Bristol

Printed and bound in Great Britain by Bell & Bain Limited, Glasgow, UK

ONTENTS

Note   Main Options A to G and secondary Options X5, X6, X8 to X11, X15, X16, X18, X19 and Y(UK)2 used in other NEC3 contracts are not used in this contract.

FOREWORD

I was delighted to be asked to write the Foreword for the NEC3 Contracts.

I have followed the outstanding rise and success of NEC contracts for a number of years now, in particular during my tenure as the 146th President of the Institution of Civil Engineers, 2010/11.

In my position as UK Government's Chief Construction Adviser, I am working with Government and industry to ensure Britain's construction sector is equipped with the knowledge, skills and best practice it needs in its transition to a low carbon economy. I am promoting innovation in the sector, including in particular the use of Building Information Modelling (BIM) in public sector construction procurement; and the synergy and fit with the collaborative nature of NEC contracts is obvious. The Government's construction strategy is a very significant investment and NEC contracts will play an important role in setting high standards of contract preparation, management and the desirable behaviour of our industry.

In the UK, we are faced with having to deliver a 15–20 per cent reduction in the cost to the public sector of construction during the lifetime of this Parliament. Shifting mind-set, attitude and behaviour into best practice NEC processes will go a considerable way to achieving this.

Of course, NEC contracts are used successfully around the world in both public and private sector projects; this trend seems set to continue at an increasing pace. NEC contracts are, according to my good friend and NEC's creator Dr Martin Barnes CBE, about better management of projects. This is quite achievable and I encourage you to understand NEC contracts to the best you can and exploit the potential this offers us all.

Peter Hansford

UK Government's Chief Construction Adviser
Cabinet Office

The NEC contracts are the only suite of standard contracts designed to facilitate and encourage good management of the projects on which they are used. The experience of using NEC contracts around the world is that they really make a difference. Previously, standard contracts were written mainly as legal documents best left in the desk drawer until costly and delaying problems had occurred and there were lengthy arguments about who was to blame.

The language of NEC contracts is clear and simple, and the procedures set out are all designed to stimulate good management. Foresighted collaboration between all the contributors to the project is the aim. The contracts set out how the interfaces between all the organisations involved will be managed – from the client through the designers and main contractors to all the many subcontractors and suppliers.

Versions of the NEC contract are specific to the work of professional service providers such as project managers and designers, to main contractors, to subcontractors and to suppliers. The wide range of situations covered by the contracts means that they do not need to be altered to suit any particular situation.

The NEC contracts are the first to deal specifically and effectively with management of the inevitable risks and uncertainties which are encountered to some extent on all projects. Management of the expected is easy, effective management of the unexpected draws fully on the collaborative approach inherent in the NEC contracts.

Most people working on projects using the NEC contracts for the first time are hugely impressed by the difference between the confrontational characteristics of traditional contracts and the teamwork engendered by the NEC. The NEC does not include specific provisions for dispute avoidance. They are not necessary. Collaborative management itself is designed to avoid disputes and it really works.

It is common for the final account for the work on a project to be settled at the time when the work is finished. The traditional long period of expensive professional work after completion to settle final payments just is not needed.

The NEC contracts are truly a massive change for the better for the industries in which they are used.

Dr Martin Barnes CBE

Originator of the NEC contracts

YOU ARE READING THE
SUPPLY CONTRACT

ACKNOWLEDGEMENTS

The first edition of the Supply Contract was produced by the Institution of Civil Engineers through its NEC Panel. It was mainly drafted by P. A. Baird and J. J. Lofty with the assistance of P. Higgins, N. C. Shaw and J. M. Hawkins.

The original NEC was designed and drafted by Dr Martin Barnes then of Coopers and Lybrand with the assistance of Professor J. G. Perry then of the University of Birmingham, T. W. Weddell then of Travers Morgan Management, T. H. Nicholson, Consultant to the Institution of Civil Engineers, A. Norman then of the University of Manchester Institute of Science and Technology and P. A. Baird, then Corporate Contracts Consultant, Eskom, South Africa.

The members of the NEC Panel are:

    N. C. Shaw, FCIPS, CEng, MIMechE (Chairman)
    F. Alderson, BA (Melb), Solicitor
    P. A. Baird, BSc, CEng, FICE, M(SA)ICE, MAPM
    M. Codling, BSc, ICIOB, MAPM
    L. T. Eames, BSc, FRICS, FCIOB
    M. Garratt, BSc(Hons), MRICS, FCIArb
    J. J. Lofty, MRICS

NEC Consultant:

    R. A. Gerrard BSc(Hons), FRICS, FCIArb, FCInstCES

Secretariat

    J. M. Hawkins, BA(Hons), MSc
    S. Hernandez, BSc, MSc

AMENDMENTS APRIL 2013

The following amendments have been made to the December 2009 edition. Full details of all amendments are available on www.neccontract.com.

Page	Clause	Line	
11	40.1	1	replace: 'The subclauses in this clause only apply' with 'This clause only applies'
16	61.1	1	text replaced
	61.3	1	text replaced
	61.4	1	text replaced
17	62.6	2	replace: 'to this effect' with 'of his failure'
	63.2	1	text replaced: first paragraph
19	64.4	2	replace: 'to this effect' with 'of his failure'
25	91.4	1	text replaced
34	Y(UK)1	1	insert new clause: 'Project Bank Account'
35	Y(UK)1	1	insert new clause: 'Trust Deed'
36	Y(UK)1	1	insert new clause: 'Joining Deed'
38	Contract Data part one	2	date replaced with: 'April 2013'
42	Y(UK)3	1	text inserted
43	Y(UK)1 and Y(UK)3	1	text inserted
44	Y(UK)1		last paragraph: text inserted

SCHEDULE OF OPTIONS

The form of contract is the core clauses and the following Options should then be considered. It is not necessary to use any of them. Any combination other than those stated may be used.

Option X1	Price adjustment for inflation
Option X2	Changes in the law
Option X3	Multiple currencies
Option X4	Parent company guarantee
Option X7	Delay damages
Option X12	Partnering
Option X13	Performance bond
Option X14	Advanced payment to the *Supplier*
Option X17	Low performance damages
Option X20	Key Performance Indicators (not used with Option X12)

The following Options dealing with national legislation should be included if required.

Option Y(UK)1	Project Back Account
Option Y(UK)3	The Contracts (Rights of Third Parties) Act 1999
Option Z	*Additional conditions of contract*
Note	Options A to G, X5, X6, X8 to X11, X15, X16, X18, X19 and Y(UK)2 are not used.

CORE CLAUSES

1 General

Actions	**10**	
	10.1	The *Purchaser*, the *Supplier* and the *Supply Manager* shall act as stated in this contract and in a spirit of mutual trust and co-operation.
Identified and defined terms	**11**	
	11.1	In these conditions of contract, terms identified in the Contract Data are in italics and defined terms have capital initials.

11.2 (1) The Accepted Programme is the programme identified in the Contract Data or is the latest programme accepted by the *Supply Manager*. The latest programme accepted by the *Supply Manager* supersedes previous Accepted Programmes.

(2) The Contract Date is the date when this contract came into existence.

(3) A Defect is

- a part of the *goods* or *services* which is not in accordance with the Goods Information or
- a part of the *goods* designed by the *Supplier* which is not in accordance with the applicable law or the *Supplier*'s design which the *Supply Manager* has accepted.

(4) Defined Cost is an amount paid by the *Supplier* in Providing the Goods and Services (excluding any tax which the *Supplier* can recover) for

- people,
- equipment,
- plant and materials to be included in the *goods* and
- transport

whether work is subcontracted or not excluding the cost of preparing quotations for compensation events.

(5) Delivery is when the *Supplier* has

- done all the work which the Goods Information states he is to do by the Delivery Date and
- corrected Defects which would have prevented the *Purchaser* from using the *goods* or *services* or Others from doing their work.

(6) The Delivery Date is the *delivery date* unless later changed in accordance with this contract.

(7) The Delivery Place is the delivery place stated in the Supply Requirements.

(8) Goods Information is information which

- specifies and describes the *goods* and *services* and
- states any constraints on how the *Supplier* Provides the Goods and Services

core
clauses

option
clauses

contract
data

and is in

- the documents which the Contract Data states it is in,
- the Supply Requirements or
- an instruction given in accordance with this contract.

(9) Others are people or organisations who are not the *Purchaser*, the *Supply Manager*, the *Adjudicator* the *Supplier* or any employee, Subcontractor or supplier of the *Supplier*.

(10) The Parties are the *Purchaser* and the *Supplier*.

(11) The Prices are the amounts stated in the price column of the Price Schedule. Where a quantity is stated for an item in the Price Schedule, the Price is calculated by multiplying the quantity by the rate.

(12) The Price Schedule is the *price schedule* unless later changed in accordance with this contract.

(13) To Provide the Goods and Services means to do the work necessary to supply the *goods* and *services* in accordance with this contract and all incidental work, services and actions which this contract requires.

(14) The Risk Register is a register of the risks which are listed in the Contract Data and the risks which the *Supply Manager* or the *Supplier* has notified as an early warning matter. It includes a description of the risk and a description of the actions to be taken to avoid or reduce the risk.

(15) A Subcontractor is a person or organisation who has a contract with the *Supplier* to

- supply part of the *goods* and *services* or
- provide plant and materials which the person or organisation has wholly or partly designed specifically for the *goods*.

(16) Supply Requirements is information which

- describes the *Purchaser*'s requirements in connection with the supply of the *goods*,
- states the delivery place,
- describes the requirements for transport of the *goods* and
- describes other information to be provided by the *Supplier* in connection with the supply of the *goods*.

Interpretation and the law 12

12.1 In this contract, except where the context shows otherwise, words in the singular also mean in the plural and the other way around and words in the masculine also mean in the feminine and neuter.

12.2 This contract is governed by the *law of the contract*.

12.3 No change to this contract, unless provided for by the *conditions of contract*, has effect unless it is has been agreed, confirmed in writing and signed by the Parties.

12.4 This contract is the entire agreement between the Parties.

12.5 In these *conditions of contract*, each reference and clause relevant to Delivery and the Delivery Date applies to each Delivery and its Delivery Date.

Communications 13

13.1 Each instruction, certificate, submission, proposal, record, acceptance, notification, reply and other communication which this contract requires is communicated in a form which can be read, copied and recorded. Writing is in the *language of this contract*.

13.2 A communication has effect when it is received at the last address notified by the recipient for receiving communications or, if none is notified, at the address of the recipient stated in the Contract Data.

13.3   If this contract requires the *Supply Manager* or the *Supplier* to reply to a communication, unless otherwise stated in this contract, he replies within the *period for reply*.

13.4   The *Supply Manager* replies to a communication submitted or resubmitted to him by the *Supplier* for acceptance. If his reply is not acceptance, the *Supply Manager* states his reasons and the *Supplier* resubmits the communication within the *period for reply* taking account of these reasons. A reason for withholding acceptance is that more information is needed in order to assess the *Supplier*'s submission fully.

13.5   The *Supply Manager* may extend the *period for reply* to a communication if the *Supply Manager* and the *Supplier* agree to the extension before the reply is due. The *Supply Manager* notifies the *Supplier* of the extension which has been agreed.

13.6   The *Supply Manager* issues his certificates to the *Supplier* and the *Purchaser*.

13.7   A notification which this contract requires is communicated separately from other communications.

13.8   The *Supply Manager* may withhold acceptance of a submission by the *Supplier*. Withholding acceptance for a reason stated in this contract is not a compensation event.

The *Supply Manager*   14

14.1   The *Supply Manager*'s acceptance of a communication from the *Supplier* or of his work does not change the *Supplier*'s responsibility to Provide the Goods and Services or his liability for his design.

14.2   The *Supply Manager*, after notifying the *Supplier*, may delegate any of his actions and may cancel any delegation. A reference to an action of the *Supply Manager* in this contract includes an action by his delegate.

14.3   The *Supply Manager* may give an instruction to the *Supplier* which changes the Goods Information.

14.4   The *Purchaser* may replace the *Supply Manager* after he has notified the *Supplier* of the name of the replacement.

Disclosure   15

15.1   The Parties and the *Supply Manager* do not disclose information obtained in connection with this contract except when necessary to carry out their duties under this contract.

Early warning   16

16.1   The *Supplier* and the *Supply Manager* give an early warning by notifying the other as soon as either becomes aware of any matter which could

- increase the total of the Prices,
- delay Delivery,
- impair the performance of the *goods* in use or
- impair the usefulness of the *services* to the *Purchaser*.

The *Supplier* may give an early warning by notifying the *Supply Manager* of any other matter which could increase his total cost. The *Supply Manager* enters early warning matters in the Risk Register. Early warning of a matter for which a compensation event has previously been notified is not required.

16.2   Either the *Supply Manager* or the *Supplier* may instruct the other to attend a risk reduction meeting. Each may instruct other people to attend if the other agrees.

core clauses

option clauses

contract data

16.3   At a risk reduction meeting, those who attend co-operate in

- making and considering proposals for how the effect of the registered risks can be avoided or reduced,
- seeking solutions that will bring advantage to all those who will be affected,
- deciding on the actions which will be taken and who, in accordance with this contract, will take them and
- deciding which risks have now been avoided or have passed and can be removed from the Risk Register.

16.4   The *Supply Manager* revises the Risk Register to record the decisions made at each risk reduction meeting and issues the revised Risk Register to the *Supplier*. If a decision needs a change to the Goods Information, the *Supply Manager* instructs the change at the same time as he issues the revised Risk Register.

Ambiguities and inconsistencies   **17**

17.1   The *Supply Manager* or the *Supplier* notifies the other as soon as either becomes aware of an ambiguity or inconsistency in or between the documents which are part of this contract. The *Supply Manager* gives an instruction resolving the ambiguity or inconsistency.

Illegal and impossible requirements   **18**

18.1   The *Supplier* notifies the *Supply Manager* as soon as he considers that the Goods Information requires him to do anything which is illegal or impossible. If the *Supply Manager* agrees, he gives an instruction to change the Goods Information appropriately.

Prevention   **19**

19.1   If an event occurs during transport of the *goods* to the Delivery Place which

- stops Delivery or
- stops Delivery by the Delivery Date,

and which

- neither Party could prevent and
- an experienced supplier would have judged at the Contract Date to have such a small chance of occurring that it would have been unreasonable for him to have allowed for it,

the *Supply Manager* gives an instruction to the *Supplier* stating how he is to deal with the event.

2 The *Supplier*'s main responsibilities

Providing the Goods
and Services **20**

20.1   The *Supplier* Provides the Goods and Services in accordance with the Goods Information.

The *Supplier*'s design **21**

21.1   The *Supplier* designs the *goods* and *services* except for those parts which the Goods Information states the *Purchaser* designs.

21.2   The *Supplier* submits the particulars of his design which the Goods Information requires to the *Supply Manager* for acceptance. A reason for not accepting the *Supplier*'s particulars is that they do not comply with either the Goods Information or the applicable law.

The *Supplier* does not proceed with the relevant work until the *Supply Manager* has accepted the particulars of his design.

21.3   The *Supplier* may submit particulars of his design for acceptance in parts if each part can be assessed fully.

Using the *Supplier*'s design
and *services* **22**

22.1   The *Purchaser* may use and copy the *Supplier*'s design and use the *services* for any purpose connected with use or alteration of the *goods* and *services* unless otherwise stated in the Goods Information and for other purposes as stated in the Goods Information.

Working with the
***Purchaser* and Others** **23**

23.1   The *Supplier* co-operates with Others in obtaining and providing information which they need in connection with the *goods* and *services*.

23.2   The *Purchaser* and the *Supplier* provide services and other things in accordance with the Goods Information. Any cost incurred by the *Purchaser* as a result of the *Supplier* not providing the services and other things which he is to provide is assessed by the *Supply Manager* and paid by the *Supplier*.

Subcontracting **24**

24.1   If the *Supplier* subcontracts work, he is responsible for Providing the Goods and Services as if he had not subcontracted. This contract applies as if a Subcontractor's employees and equipment were the *Supplier*'s.

24.2   The *Supplier* submits the name of each proposed Subcontractor to the *Supply Manager* for acceptance. A reason for not accepting the Subcontractor is that his appointment will not allow the *Supplier* to Provide the Goods and Services. The *Supplier* does not appoint a proposed Subcontractor until the *Supply Manager* has accepted him.

Other responsibilities **25**

25.1   The *Supplier* obtains approval of his design from Others where necessary.

25.2   The *Supplier* provides access to work being done for this contract for

- the *Supply Manager* and
- Others notified to him by the *Supply Manager*

subject to the restrictions stated in the Contract Data. The *Supplier* may not restrict the *Supply Manager*'s right to watch any test done by the *Supplier* which is required by the Goods Information or the applicable law.

25.3   The *Supplier* obeys an instruction which is in accordance with this contract and is given to him by the *Supply Manager*.

core
clauses

option
clauses

contract
data

25.4 The *Supplier* acts in accordance with the health and safety requirement stated in the Goods Information.

25.5 The *Supplier* obtains permission from Others where necessary before transporting the *goods* to the Delivery Place.

3 Time

Starting and Delivery **30**

30.1 The *Supplier* does not start work until the *starting date* and does the work so that Delivery is on or before the Delivery Date.

30.2 The *Supplier* does not bring the *goods* to the Delivery Place more than one week before the Delivery Date if it is stated in the Contract Data that he may not do so.

The programme **31**

31.1 If a programme is not identified in the Contract Data, the *Supplier* submits a first programme to the *Supply Manager* for acceptance within the period stated in the Contract Data.

31.2 The *Supplier* shows on each programme which he submits for acceptance

- the *starting date* and Delivery Date,
- planned Delivery,
- the dates when, in order to Provide the Goods and Services, the *Supplier* will need

  - access to the *Purchaser*'s premises,
  - acceptances and
  - plant and materials and other things to be provided by the *Purchaser*,

- the dates when the *Supplier* plans to conduct factory acceptance tests or inspections and
- other information which the Goods Information requires the *Supplier* to show on a programme.

31.3 Within two weeks of the *Supplier* submitting a programme to him for acceptance, the *Supply Manager* either accepts the programme or notifies the *Supplier* of his reasons for not accepting it. A reason for not accepting a programme is that

- the *Supplier*'s plans which it shows are not practicable,
- it does not show the information which this contract requires,
- it does not represent the *Supplier*'s plans realistically or
- it does not comply with the Goods Information.

Revising the programme **32**

32.1 The *Supplier* shows on each revised programme

- the actual progress achieved on each operation and its effect upon the timing of the remaining work,
- the effects of implemented compensation events,
- how the *Supplier* plans to deal with any delays and to correct notified Defects and
- any other changes which the *Supplier* proposes to make to the Accepted Programme.

32.2 The *Supplier* submits a revised programme to the *Supply Manager* for acceptance

- within the *period for reply* after the *Supply Manager* has instructed him to,
- when the *Supplier* chooses to and, in any case,
- at no longer interval than the interval stated in the Contract Data from the *starting date* until Delivery of the whole of the *goods* and *services*.

Access **33**

33.1 The *Purchaser* allows access to and use of his premises to the *Supplier* as necessary for the work included in this contract.

core clauses

option clauses

contract data

Instructions to stop or **34**
not to start work 34.1 The *Supply Manager* may instruct the *Supplier* to stop or not to start any wor and may later instruct him to re-start or start it.

Acceleration **35**
35.1 The *Supply Manager* may instruct the *Supplier* to submit a quotation for a acceleration to achieve Delivery before the Delivery Date. A quotation for a acceleration comprises proposed changes to the Prices and the Delivery Date The *Supplier* submits details of his assessment with each quotation.

35.2 The *Supplier* submits a quotation or gives his reasons for not doing so withi the *period for reply*. When the *Supply Manager* accepts a quotation for a acceleration, he changes the Prices and the Delivery Date accordingly.

4 Testing and Defects

Tests and inspections **40**

40.1   This clause only applies to tests and inspections required by the Goods Information or the applicable law.

40.2   The *Supplier* and the *Purchaser* provide records, data sheets, materials, facilities and samples for tests and inspections as stated in the Goods Information.

40.3   The *Supplier* and the *Supply Manager* each notifies the other of each of his tests and inspections before it starts and afterwards notifies the other of its results. The *Supplier* notifies the *Supply Manager* in time for a test or inspection to be arranged and done before doing work which would obstruct the test or inspection. The *Supply Manager* may watch any test done by the *Supplier*.

40.4   If a test or inspection shows that any work has a Defect, the *Supplier* corrects the Defect and the test or inspection is repeated.

40.5   The *Supply Manager* does his tests and inspections without causing unnecessary delay to the work or to a payment which is conditional upon a test or inspection being successful.

40.6   The *Supply Manager* assesses the cost incurred by the *Purchaser* when a test or inspection is repeated after a Defect is found. The *Supplier* pays the amount assessed.

Testing and inspection before Delivery **41**

41.1   The *Supplier* does not bring to the Delivery Place those *goods* which the Goods Information states are to be tested or inspected before being brought to the Delivery Place until

- the *Supply Manager* has notified the *Supplier* that they have passed the test or inspection which the *Supply Manager* is to do and
- the *Supplier* has notified the *Supply Manager* that they have passed the test or inspection which the *Supplier* is to do.

Searching for and notifying Defects **42**

42.1   Until the *defects date* for the *goods* and *services* included in Delivery, the *Supply Manager* may instruct the *Supplier* to search for a Defect in the *goods* and *services* included in the Delivery. He gives his reason for the search with his instruction.

42.2   Until the *defects date* for the *goods* and *services* included in Delivery, the *Supply Manager* notifies the *Supplier* of each Defect as soon as he becomes aware of it and the *Supplier* notifies the *Supply Manager* of each Defect as soon as he becomes aware of it.

Correcting Defects **43**

43.1   The *Supplier* corrects a Defect whether or not the *Supply Manager* notifies him of it.

43.2   After Delivery, the *Supplier* corrects a notified Defect before the end of the *defect correction period*. The *defect correction period* begins when the *Supply Manager* has arranged the access necessary for the *Supplier* to correct the Defect.

43.3   After Delivery, the *Purchaser* allows access to correct a notified Defect within the *defect access period* following notification. The *Supplier* is not liable for any damage to the *goods* or *services* resulting from a failure by the *Purchaser* to provide access to correct a notified Defect later than the end of the *defect access period* following notification.

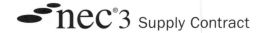

Accepting Defects **44**

44.1 The *Supplier* and the *Supply Manager* may propose to the other that the Goods Information should be changed so that a Defect does not have to be corrected.

44.2 If the *Supplier* and the *Supply Manager* are prepared to consider the change, the *Supplier* submits a quotation for reduced Prices or an earlier Delivery Date or both to the *Supply Manager* for acceptance. If the *Supply Manager* accepts the quotation, he gives an instruction to change the Goods Information, the Prices and the Delivery Date accordingly.

Uncorrected Defects **45**

45.1 If the *Supplier* is given access in order to correct a notified Defect but he has not corrected it within its *defect correction period*, the *Supply Manager* assesses the cost to the *Purchaser* of having the Defect corrected by other people and the *Supplier* pays this amount. The Goods Information is treated as having been changed to accept the Defect.

45.2 If the *Supplier* is not given access in order to correct a notified Defect before the *defects date*, the *Supply Manager* assesses the cost to the *Supplier* of correcting the Defect at the time it was notified and the *Supplier* pays this amount. The Goods Information is treated as having been changed to accept the Defect.

core clauses

option clauses

contract data

5 Payment

Assessing the amount due	**50**

50.1   The *Supply Manager* assesses the amount due at each assessment date. The first assessment date is decided by the *Supply Manager* to suit the procedures of the Parties and is not later than the *assessment interval* after the *starting date.* Later assessment dates occur at the end of each *assessment interval* until four weeks after the last *defects date.*

50.2   The amount due is

- the Price for each lump sum item in the Price Schedule which the *Supplier* has completed,
- where a quantity is stated for an item in the Price Schedule, an amount calculated by multiplying the quantity which the *Supplier* has completed by the rate,
- plus other amounts to be paid to the *Supplier,*
- less amounts to be paid by or retained from the *Supplier.*

Any tax which the law requires the *Purchaser* to pay to the *Supplier* is included in the amount due.

50.3   In assessing the amount due, the *Supply Manager* considers any application for payment the *Supplier* has submitted on or before the assessment date. The *Supply Manager* gives the *Supplier* details of how the amount due has been assessed.

50.4   The *Supply Manager* corrects any wrongly assessed amount due in a later payment certificate.

Payment	**51**

51.1   The *Supply Manager* certifies a payment within one week of each assessment date. The first payment is the amount due. Other payments are the change in the amount due since the last payment certificate. A payment is made by the *Supplier* to the *Purchaser* if the change reduces the amount due. Other payments are made by the *Purchaser* to the *Supplier.* Payments are in the *currency of this contract* unless otherwise stated in this contract.

51.2   Each certified payment is made within three weeks of the assessment date or, if a different period is stated in the Contract Data, within the period stated. If a certified payment is late, or if the payment is late because the *Supply Manager* does not issue a certificate which he should issue, interest is paid on the late payment. Interest is assessed from the date by which the late payment should have been made until the date when the late payment is made, and is included in the first assessment after the late payment is made.

51.3   If an amount due is corrected in a later certificate either

- by the *Supply Manager* in relation to a mistake or a compensation event or
- following a decision of the *Adjudicator* or the *tribunal,*

interest on the correcting amount is paid. Interest is assessed from the date when the incorrect amount was certified until the date when the correcting amount is certified and is included in the assessment which includes the correcting amount.

51.4   Interest is calculated on a daily basis at the *interest rate* and is compounded annually.

Defined Cost **52**

52.1 All the *Supplier*'s costs which are not included in the Defined Cost are treated as included in the *percentage for overheads and profit*. Defined Cost include only amounts calculated at open market or competitively tendered prices with deductions for all discounts, rebates and taxes which can be recovered.

The Price Schedule **53**

53.1 Information in the Price Schedule is not Goods Information.

core clauses

option clauses

contract data

6 Compensation events

Compensation events   60

60.1   The following are compensation events.

(1) The *Supply Manager* gives an instruction changing the Goods Information except

- a change made in order to accept a Defect or
- a change to the Goods Information provided by the *Supplier* for his design which is made either at his request or to comply with other Goods Information provided by the *Purchaser*.

(2) The *Purchaser* does not allow access to and use of the parts of the *Purchaser*'s premises necessary for the work included in this contract by the later of the date when the access becomes necessary and the date shown on the Accepted Programme.

(3) The *Purchaser* does not provide something which he is to provide by the date for providing it shown on the Accepted Programme.

(4) The *Supply Manager* gives an instruction to stop or not to start any work.

(5) The *Purchaser* or people acting on behalf of the *Purchaser* do not work within the conditions stated in the Goods Information.

(6) The *Supply Manager* does not reply to a communication from the *Supplier* within the period required by this contract.

(7) The *Supply Manager* changes a decision which he has previously communicated to the *Supplier*.

(8) The *Supply Manager* withholds an acceptance (other than acceptance of a quotation for an acceleration or for not correcting a Defect) for a reason not stated in this contract.

(9) The *Supply Manager* instructs the *Supplier* to search for a Defect and no Defect is found unless the search is needed only because the *Supplier* gave insufficient notice of doing work obstructing a required test or inspection.

(10) A test or inspection done by the *Supply Manager* causes unnecessary delay.

(11) The *Purchaser* does not provide records, data sheets, materials, facilities and samples for tests and inspections as stated in the Goods Information.

(12) An event which is a *Purchaser*'s risk stated in this contract.

(13) The *Supply Manager* notifies a correction to an assumption which he has previously stated about a compensation event.

(14) A breach of contract by the *Purchaser* which is not one of the other compensation events in this contract.

(15) An event occurs during transport of the *goods* to the Delivery Place which

- stops Delivery or
- stops Delivery by the Delivery Date,

and which

- neither Party could prevent,
- an experienced supplier would have judged at the Contract Date to have such a small chance of occurring that it would have been unreasonable for him to have allowed for it and
- is not one of the other compensation events stated in this contract.

Notifying compensation events	**61**	
	61.1	For compensation events which arise from the *Supply Manager* giving an instruction, changing an earlier decision or correcting an assumption, the *Supply Manager* notifies the *Supplier* of the compensation event at the time of that communication. He also instructs the *Supplier* to submit quotations, unless the event arises from a fault of the *Supplier* or quotations have already been submitted. The *Supplier* puts the instruction or changed decision into effect.

61.2 The *Supply Manager* may instruct the *Supplier* to submit quotations for a proposed instruction or a proposed changed decision. The *Supplier* does not put a proposed instruction or a proposed changed decision into effect.

61.3 The *Supplier* notifies the *Supply Manager* of an event which has happened or which he expects to happen as a compensation event if

- the *Supplier* believes that the event is a compensation event and
- the *Supply Manager* has not notified the event to the *Supplier*.

If the *Supplier* does not notify a compensation event within eight weeks of becoming aware of the event, he is not entitled to a change in the Prices or the Delivery Date unless the event arises from the *Supply Manager* giving an instruction, changing an earlier decision or correcting an assumption.

61.4 If the *Supply Manager* decides that an event notified by the *Supplier*

- arises from a fault of the *Supplier*,
- has not happened and is not expected to happen,
- has no effect upon Defined Cost or Delivery or
- is not one of the compensation events stated in this contract

he notifies the *Supplier* of his decision that the Prices and the Delivery Date are not to be changed. If the *Supply Manager* decides otherwise, he notifies the *Supplier* accordingly and instructs him to submit quotations.

The *Supply Manager* notifies his decision to the *Supplier* and, if his decision is that the Prices and the Delivery Date are to be changed, instructs him to submit quotations before the end of either

- one week after the *Supplier*'s notification or
- a longer period to which the *Supplier* has agreed.

If the *Supply Manager* does not notify his decision, the *Supplier* may notify the *Supply Manager* of his failure. A failure by the *Supply Manager* to reply within two weeks of this notification is treated as acceptance by the *Supply Manager* that the event is a compensation event and an instruction to submit quotations.

61.5 If the *Supply Manager* decides that the *Supplier* did not give an early warning of the event which an experienced supplier could have given, he notifies this decision to the *Supplier* when he instructs him to submit quotations.

61.6 If the *Supply Manager* decides that the effects of a compensation event are too uncertain to be forecast reasonably, he states assumptions about the event in his instruction to the *Supplier* to submit quotations. Assessment o the event is based on these assumptions. If any of them is later found to have been wrong, the *Supply Manager* notifies a correction.

61.7 A compensation event is not notified after the last *defects date*.

Quotations for compensation events	**62**	
	62.1	After discussing with the *Supplier* different ways of dealing with the compensation event which are practicable, the *Supply Manager* may instruct the *Supplier* to submit alternative quotations. The *Supplier* submits the required quotations to the *Supply Manager* and may submit quotations for other methods of dealing with the compensation event which he considers practicable.

62.2 Quotations for compensation events comprise proposed changes to the Prices and any delay to the Delivery Date assessed by the *Supplier*. The *Supplier* submits details of his assessment with each quotation. If the *Supplier*'s programme for remaining work is altered by the compensation event, the *Supplier* includes the alterations to the Accepted Programme in his quotation.

62.3   The *Supplier* submits quotations within three weeks of being instructed to do so by the *Supply Manager*. The *Supply Manager* replies within two weeks of the submission. His reply is

- an instruction to submit a revised quotation,
- an acceptance of a quotation,
- a notification that a proposed instruction will not be given or a proposed changed decision will not be made or
- a notification that he will be making his own assessment.

62.4   The *Supply Manager* instructs the *Supplier* to submit a revised quotation only after explaining his reasons for doing so to the *Supplier*. The *Supplier* submits the revised quotation within three weeks of being instructed to do so.

62.5   The *Supply Manager* extends the time allowed for

- the *Supplier* to submit quotations for a compensation event and
- the *Supply Manager* to reply to a quotation

if the *Supply Manager* and the *Supplier* agree to the extension before the submission or reply is due. The *Supply Manager* notifies the extension that has been agreed to the *Supplier*.

62.6   If the *Supply Manager* does not reply to a quotation within the time allowed, the *Supplier* may notify the *Supply Manager* of his failure. If the *Supplier* submitted more than one quotation for the compensation event, he states in his notification which quotation he proposes is to be accepted. If the *Supply Manager* does not reply to the notification within two weeks, and unless the quotation is for a proposed instruction or a proposed changed decision, the *Supplier*'s notification is treated as acceptance of the quotation by the *Supply Manager*.

Assessing compensation   63
events   63.1   If the *Supply Manager* and the *Supplier* agree, for a compensation event which only affects the quantities of *goods* and *services* shown in the Price Schedule, the change to the Prices is assessed by multiplying the changed quantities by the appropriate rates in the Price Schedule.

63.2   For other compensation events, the changes to the Prices are assessed as the effect of the compensation event upon

- the actual Defined Cost of the work already done,
- the forecast Defined Cost of the work not yet done and
- the resulting amount calculated by applying the *percentage for overheads and profit* to the Defined Cost of the work.

Effects on Defined Cost are assessed separately for

- people,
- equipment,
- plant and materials included in the *goods*,
- work subcontracted by the *Supplier* and
- transport.

The *Supplier* shows how each of these effects is built up in each quotation for a compensation event.

If the compensation event arose from the *Supply Manager* giving an instruction, changing an earlier decision or correcting an assumption, the date which divides the work already done from the work not yet done is the date of that communication. In all other cases, the date is the date of the notification of the compensation event.

The *percentage for overheads and profit* is applied to the assessed effect of the event on Defined Cost except that it is not applied to any tax charges for

- customs clearance and
- export and import.

The date when the *Supply Manager* instructed or should have instructed the *Supplier* to submit quotations divides the work already done from the work not yet done.

63.3 If the effect of a compensation event is to reduce the total Defined Cost, the Prices are not reduced except as stated in this contract.

63.4 A delay to the Delivery Date is assessed as the length of time that, due to the compensation event, planned Delivery is later than planned Delivery as shown on the Accepted Programme.

63.5 The rights of the *Purchaser* and the *Supplier* to changes to the Prices and the Delivery Date are their only rights in respect of a compensation event.

63.6 If the *Supply Manager* has notified the *Supplier* of his decision that the *Supplier* did not give an early warning of a compensation event which an experienced supplier could have given, the event is assessed as if the *Supplier* had given early warning.

63.7 Assessment of the effect of a compensation event includes risk allowances for cost and time for matters which have a significant chance of occurring and are at the *Supplier*'s risk under this contract.

63.8 Assessments are based upon the assumptions that the *Supplier* reacts competently and promptly to the compensation event, that any Defined Cost and time due to the event are reasonably incurred and that the *Supplier*'s Accepted Programme can be changed.

63.9 A compensation event which is an instruction to change the Goods Information in order to resolve an ambiguity or inconsistency is assessed as if the Prices and the Delivery Date were for the interpretation most favourable to the Party which did not provide the Goods Information.

63.10 If the effect of a compensation event is to reduce the total Defined Cost and the event is

- a change to the Goods Information or
- a correction of an assumption stated by the *Supply Manager* for assessing an earlier compensation event,

the Prices are reduced.

63.11 Assessments for changed Prices for compensation events are in the form of changes to the Price Schedule.

63.12 If the *Supply Manager* and the *Supplier* agree, rates and lump sums may be used to assess a compensation event instead of Defined Cost.

The *Supply Manager*'s 64
assessments 64.1 The *Supply Manager* assesses a compensation event

- if the *Supplier* has not submitted a quotation and details of his assessment within the time allowed,
- if the *Supply Manager* decides that the *Supplier* has not assessed the compensation event correctly in a quotation and he does not instruct the *Supplier* to submit a revised quotation,
- if, when the *Supplier* submits quotations for a compensation event, he has not submitted a programme or alterations to a programme which this contract requires him to submit or
- if, when the *Supplier* submits quotations for a compensation event, the *Supply Manager* has not accepted the *Supplier*'s latest programme for one of the reasons stated in this contract.

core clauses

option clauses

contract data

64.2 The *Supply Manager* assesses a compensation event using his own assessment of the programme for the remaining work if

- there is no Accepted Programme or
- the *Supplier* has not submitted a programme or alterations to a programme for acceptance as required by this contract.

64.3 The *Supply Manager* notifies the *Supplier* of his assessment of a compensation event and gives him details of it within the period allowed for the *Supplier*'s submission of his quotation for the same event. This period starts when the need for the *Supply Manager*'s assessment becomes apparent.

64.4 If the *Supply Manager* does not assess a compensation event within the time allowed, the *Supplier* may notify the *Supply Manager* of his failure. If the *Supplier* submitted more than one quotation for the compensation event, he states in his notification which quotation he proposes is to be accepted. If the *Supply Manager* does not reply within two weeks of this notification the notification is treated as acceptance of the *Supplier*'s quotation by the *Supply Manager*.

Implementing
compensation events **65**

65.1 A compensation event is implemented when

- the *Supply Manager* notifies his acceptance of the *Supplier*'s quotation,
- the *Supply Manager* notifies the *Supplier* of his own assessment or
- a *Supplier*'s quotation is treated as having been accepted by the *Supply Manager*.

65.2 The assessment of a compensation event is not revised if a forecast upon which it is based is shown by later recorded information to have been wrong.

65.3 The changes to the Prices and the Delivery Date are included in the notification implementing a compensation event.

core
clauses

option
clauses

contract
data

7 Title

<table>
<tr>
<td>The Purchaser's title
to the goods</td>
<td>70</td>
<td></td>
</tr>
<tr>
<td></td>
<td>70.1</td>
<td>Title to the goods passes to the Purchaser when payment for the goods which this contract requires has been made.</td>
</tr>
<tr>
<td></td>
<td>70.2</td>
<td>Before payment for the goods is made, the Supplier provides information to the Purchaser to show that he is able to pass title to the goods.</td>
</tr>
<tr>
<td>Marking goods
before Delivery</td>
<td>71</td>
<td></td>
</tr>
<tr>
<td></td>
<td>71.1</td>
<td>The Supplier marks the goods as the Goods Information requires if this contract identifies them for payment before they are brought within the Delivery Place.</td>
</tr>
</table>

core clauses

option clauses

contract data

 www.neccontract.com

8 Risks, liabilities, indemnities and insurance

Purchaser's risks   **80**

80.1   The following are *Purchaser*'s risks.

- Claims, proceedings, compensation and costs payable which are due to

  - the unavoidable result of the supply of the *goods* and *services*,
  - negligence, breach of statutory duty or interference with any legal right by the *Purchaser* or by any person employed by or contracted to him except the *Supplier* or
  - a fault of the *Purchaser* or a fault in his design.

- Loss of or damage to plant and materials supplied to the *Supplier* by the *Purchaser*, or by Others on the *Purchaser*'s behalf, until the *Supplier* has received and accepted them.

- Loss of or wear or damage to the *goods* and *services* after Delivery except loss, wear or damage occurring before the *defects date* which is due to

  - a Defect which existed at Delivery,
  - an event occurring before Delivery which is not a *Purchaser*'s risk or
  - the activities of the *Supplier* after Delivery.

- Loss of or wear or damage to the *goods* and *services* and plant and materials retained by the *Purchaser* after Delivery after a termination, except loss, wear or damage due to the activities of the *Supplier* after Delivery following the termination.

- Additional *Purchaser*'s risks stated in the Contract Data.

The *Supplier*'s risks   **81**

81.1   From the *starting date* until the last *defects date* the risks which are not carried by the *Purchaser* are carried by the *Supplier*.

Loss of and damage to the *goods*   **82**

82.1   Until the last *defects date* and unless otherwise instructed by the *Supply Manager,* the *Supplier* promptly replaces loss of and repairs damage to the *goods*.

Indemnity   **83**

83.1   Each Party indemnifies the other against claims, proceedings, compensation and costs due to an event which is at his risk.

83.2   The liability of each Party to indemnify the other is reduced if events at the other Party's risk contributed to the claims, proceedings, compensation and costs. The reduction is in proportion to the extent that events which were at the other Party's risk contributed, taking into account each Party's responsibilities under this contract.

Insurance cover   **84**

84.1   The *Supplier* provides the insurances stated in the Insurance Table except any insurance which the *Purchaser* is to provide as stated in the Contract Data. The *Supplier* provides additional insurances as stated in the Contract Data.

84.2   The insurances provide cover for events which are at the *Supplier*'s risk from the *starting date* until the last *defects date* or a termination certificate has been issued.

core clauses

option clauses

contract data

INSURANCE TABLE

Insurance against	Minimum amount of cover or minimum limit of indemnity
Loss of or damage to the *goods*, plant and materials	The replacement cost, including the amount stated in the Contract Data for the replacement of any plant and materials provided by the *Purchaser*
Liability for loss of or damage to property (except the *goods*, plant and materials and equipment) and liability for bodily injury to or death of a person (not an employee of the *Supplier*) caused by activity in connection with this contract	The amount stated in the Contract Data for any one event with cross liability so that the insurance applies to the Parties separately
Liability for death of or bodily injury to employees of the *Supplier* arising out of and in the course of their employment in connection with this contract	The greater of the amount required by the applicable law and the amount stated in the Contract Data for any one event

Insurance policies 85

85.1 Before the *starting date* and on each renewal of the insurance policy until the last *defects date* the *Supplier*, if instructed by the *Supply Manager*, submits to the *Supply Manager* for acceptance certificates which state that the insurance required by this contract is in force. The certificates are signed by the *Supplier*'s insurer or insurance broker. A reason for not accepting the certificates is that they do not comply with this contract.

85.2 Insurance policies include a waiver by the insurers of their subrogation rights against directors and other employees of every insured except where there is fraud.

85.3 The Parties comply with the terms and conditions of the insurance policies.

85.4 Any amount not recovered from an insurer is borne by the *Purchaser* for events which are at his risk and by the *Supplier* for events which are at his risk.

**If the *Supplier* 86
does not insure**

86.1 The *Purchaser* may insure a risk which this contract requires the *Supplier* to insure if the *Supplier* does not submit a required certificate. The cost of this insurance to the *Purchaser* is paid by the *Supplier*.

**Insurance by the 87
*Purchaser***

87.1 The *Supply Manager* submits policies and certificates for insurances provided by the *Purchaser* to the *Supplier* for acceptance before the *starting date* and afterwards as the *Supplier* instructs. The *Supplier* accepts the policies and certificates if they comply with this contract.

87.2 The *Supplier*'s acceptance of an insurance policy or certificate provided by the *Purchaser* does not change the responsibility of the *Purchaser* to provide the insurances stated in the Contract Data.

87.3 The *Supplier* may insure a risk which this contract requires the *Purchaser* to insure if the *Purchaser* does not submit a required policy or certificate. The cost of this insurance to the *Supplier* is paid by the *Purchaser*.

Limitation of liability **88**

88.1 The *Supplier*'s liability to the *Purchaser* for the *Purchaser*'s indirect or consequential loss, including loss of profit, revenue or goodwill, is limited to the amount stated in the Contract Data.

88.2 For any one event, the liability of the *Supplier* to the *Purchaser* for loss of or damage to the *Purchaser*'s property is limited to the amount stated in the Contract Data.

88.3 The *Supplier*'s liability to the *Purchaser* for Defects due to his design which are not notified before the last *defects date* is limited to the amount stated in the Contract Data.

88.4 The *Supplier*'s total liability to the *Purchaser* for all matters arising under or in connection with this contract, other than the excluded matters, is limited to the amount stated in the Contract Data and applies in contract, tort or delict and otherwise to the extent allowed under the *law of the contract*.

The excluded matters are amounts payable by the *Supplier* as stated in this contract for

- loss of or damage to the *Purchaser*'s property,
- delay damages if Option X7 applies and
- low performance damages if Option X17 applies.

88.5 The *Supplier* is not liable to the *Purchaser* for a matter unless it is notified to the *Supplier* before the *end of liability date*.

core clauses

option clauses

contract data

© copyright nec 2013

9 Termination and dispute resolution

Termination   **90**

90.1   If either Party wishes to terminate the *Supplier*'s obligation to Provide the Goods and Services he notifies the *Supply Manager* and the other Party giving details of his reason for terminating. The *Supply Manager* issues a termination certificate to both Parties promptly if the reason complies with this contract.

90.2   The *Supplier* may terminate only for a reason identified in the Termination Table. The *Purchaser* may terminate for any reason. The procedures followed and the amounts due on termination are in accordance with the Termination Table.

TERMINATION TABLE

Terminating Party	Reason	Procedure	Amount due
The *Purchaser*	A reason other than R1–R21	P1 and P2	A1 and A2
	R1–R15 or R18	P1, P2 and P3	A1 and A3
	R17 or R20	P1 and P3	A1 and A2
	R21	P1 and P4	A1 and A2
The *Supplier*	R1–R10, R16, R17, R19 or R20	P1 and P4	A1 and A2

90.3   The procedures for termination are implemented immediately after the *Supply Manager* has issued a termination certificate.

90.4   Within thirteen weeks of termination, the *Supply Manager* certifies a final payment to or from the *Supplier* which is the *Supply Manager*'s assessment of the amount due on termination less the total of previous payments. Payment is made within three weeks of the *Supply Manager*'s certificate.

90.5   After a termination certificate has been issued, the *Supplier* does no further work necessary to Provide the Goods and Services.

Reasons for termination   **91**

91.1   Either Party may terminate if the other Party has done one of the following or its equivalent.

- If the other Party is an individual and has
  - presented his petition for bankruptcy (R1),
  - had a bankruptcy order made against him (R2),
  - had a receiver appointed over his assets (R3) or
  - made an arrangement with his creditors (R4).

- If the other Party is a company or partnership and has
  - had a winding-up order made against it (R5),
  - had a provisional liquidator appointed to it (R6),
  - passed a resolution for winding-up (other than in order to amalgamate or reconstruct) (R7),
  - had an administration order made against it (R8),
  - had a receiver, receiver and manager, or administrative receiver appointed over the whole or a substantial part of its undertaking or assets (R9) or
  - made an arrangement with its creditors (R10).

91.2 The *Purchaser* may terminate if the *Supply Manager* has notified that the *Supplier* has defaulted in one of the following ways and not put the default right within four weeks of the notification.

- Substantially failed to comply with his obligations (R11).
- Not provided a bond or guarantee which this contract requires (R12).
- Appointed a Subcontractor for substantial work before the *Supply Manager* has accepted the Subcontractor (R13).

91.3 The *Purchaser* may terminate if the *Supply Manager* has notified that the *Supplier* has defaulted in one of the following ways and not stopped defaulting within four weeks of the notification.

- Substantially hindered the *Purchaser* or Others (R14).
- Substantially broken a health or safety regulation (R15).

91.4 The *Supplier* may terminate if the *Purchaser* has not paid an amount due under the contract within eleven weeks of the date that it should have been paid (R16).

91.5 Either Party may terminate if the Parties have been released under the law from further performance of the whole of this contract (R17).

91.6 If the *Supply Manager* has instructed the *Supplier* to stop or not to start any substantial work or all work and an instruction allowing the work to re-start or start has not been given within thirteen weeks,

- the *Purchaser* may terminate if the instruction was due to a default by the *Supplier* (R18),
- the *Supplier* may terminate if the instruction was due to a default by the *Purchaser* (R19) and
- either Party may terminate if the instruction was due to any other reason (R20).

91.7 The *Purchaser* may terminate if an event occurs which

- stops Delivery or
- stops Delivery by the Delivery Date and is forecast to delay Delivery by more than 13 weeks,

and which

- neither Party could prevent and
- an experienced supplier would have judged at the Contract Date to have such a small chance of occurring that it would have been unreasonable for him to have allowed for it (R21).

Procedures on termination 92

92.1 On termination, the *Purchaser* may obtain the remaining *goods* and *services* from other suppliers (P1).

92.2 The procedure on termination also includes one or more of the following as set out in the Termination Table.

P2 The *Purchaser* may instruct the *Supplier* to leave the *Purchaser*'s premises, remove any of his equipment, plant and materials and assign the benefit of any subcontract or other contract related to performance of this contract to the *Purchaser*.

P3 The *Purchaser* may use any equipment to which the *Supplier* has title, except equipment fixed in the *Supplier*'s premises, to complete the supply of the *goods* and *services*. The *Supplier* promptly removes the equipment when the *Supply Manager* notifies him that the *Purchaser* no longer requires it to complete the supply of the *goods* and *services*.

P4 The *Supplier* leaves the Delivery Place and removes any of his equipment which is on the *Purchaser*'s premises.

core clauses

option clauses

contract data

Payment on termination **93**

93.1 The amount due on termination includes (A1)

- an amount due assessed as for normal payments,
- the Defined Cost of *goods* and *services* not included in normal payment and reasonably incurred in expectation of completing the whole of the *goods* and *services*, less the cost of *goods* and *services* which can be resold or used elsewhere,
- any amounts retained by the *Purchaser* and
- a deduction of any un-repaid balance of an advanced payment.

93.2 The amount due on termination also includes one or more of the following as set out in the Termination Table.

A2 The forecast Defined Cost of removing the equipment.

A3 A deduction of the forecast of the additional cost to the *Purchaser* of providing the whole of the *goods* and *services*.

Dispute resolution **94**

94.1 A dispute arising under or in connection with this contract is referred to and decided by the *Adjudicator*.

The *Adjudicator* 94.2 (1) The Parties appoint the *Adjudicator* under the NEC Adjudicator's Contract current at the *starting date*.

(2) The *Adjudicator* acts impartially and decides the dispute as an independent adjudicator and not as an arbitrator.

(3) If the *Adjudicator* is not identified in the Contract Data or if the *Adjudicator* resigns or is unable to act, the Parties choose a new adjudicator jointly. If the Parties have not chosen an adjudicator, either Party may ask the *Adjudicator nominating body* to choose one. The *Adjudicator nominating body* chooses an adjudicator within four days of the request. The chosen adjudicator becomes the *Adjudicator*.

(4) A replacement *Adjudicator* has the power to decide a dispute referred to his predecessor but not decided at the time when the predecessor resigned or became unable to act. He deals with an undecided dispute as if it had been referred to him on the date he was appointed.

(5) The *Adjudicator*, his employees and agents are not liable to the Parties for any action or failure to take action in an adjudication unless the action or failure to take action was in bad faith.

The adjudication 94.3 (1) Disputes are notified and referred to the *Adjudicator* in accordance with the Adjudication Table.

ADJUDICATION TABLE

Dispute about	Which Party may refer it to the *Adjudicator*?	When may it be referred to the *Adjudicator*?
An action of the *Supply Manager*	The *Supplier*	Between two and four weeks after the *Supplier*'s notification of the dispute to the *Purchaser* and the *Supply Manager*, the notification itself being made not more than four weeks after the *Supplier* becomes aware of the action
The *Supply Manager* not having taken an action	The *Supplier*	Between two and four weeks after the *Supplier*'s notification of the dispute to the *Purchaser* and the *Supply Manager*, the notification itself being made not more than four weeks after the *Supplier* becomes aware that the action was not taken
A quotation for a compensation event which is treated as having been accepted	The *Purchaser*	Between two and four weeks after the *Supply Manager*'s notification of the dispute to the *Purchaser* and the *Supplier*, the notification itself being made not more than four weeks after the quotation was treated as accepted
Any other matter	Either Party	Between two and four weeks after notification of the dispute to the other Party and the *Supply Manager*

(2) The times for notifying and referring a dispute may be extended by the *Supply Manager* if the *Supplier* and the *Supply Manager* agree to the extension before the notice or referral is due. The *Supply Manager* notifies the extension that has been agreed to the *Supplier*. If a disputed matter is not notified and referred within the times set out in this contract, neither Party may subsequently refer it to the *Adjudicator* or the *tribunal*.

(3) The Party referring the dispute to the *Adjudicator* includes with his referral information to be considered by the *Adjudicator*. Any more information from a Party to be considered by the *Adjudicator* is provided within four weeks from the referral. This period may be extended if the *Adjudicator* and the Parties agree.

(4) If a matter disputed by the *Supplier* under or in connection with a subcontract is also a matter disputed under or in connection with this contract and if the subcontract allows, the *Supplier* may refer the subcontract dispute to the *Adjudicator* at the same time as the main contract referral. The *Adjudicator* then decides the disputes together and references to the Parties for the purposes of the dispute are interpreted as including the Subcontractor.

core clauses

option clauses

contract data

(5) The *Adjudicator* may

- review and revise any action or inaction of the *Supply Manager* related t the dispute and alter a quotation which has been treated as having bee accepted,
- take the initiative in ascertaining the facts and the law related to th dispute,
- instruct a Party to provide further information related to the disput within a stated time and
- instruct a Party to take any other action which he considers necessary t reach his decision and to do so within a stated time.

(6) A communication between a Party and the *Adjudicator* is communicated t the other Party at the same time.

(7) If the *Adjudicator*'s decision includes assessment of additional cost c delay caused to the *Supplier*, he makes his assessment in the same way as compensation event is assessed.

(8) The *Adjudicator* decides the dispute and notifies the Parties and th *Supply Manager* of his decision and his reasons within four weeks of the en of the period for receiving information. This four week period may be extende if the Parties agree.

(9) Unless and until the *Adjudicator* has notified the Parties of his decisior the Parties and the *Supply Manager* proceed as if the matter disputed wa not disputed.

(10) The *Adjudicator*'s decision is binding on the Parties unless and unt revised by the *tribunal* and is enforceable as a matter of contractual obligatio between the Parties and not as an arbitral award. The *Adjudicator*'s decisio is final and binding if neither Party has notified the other within the time required by this contract that he is dissatisfied with a decision of the *Adjud cator* and intends to refer the matter to the *tribunal*.

(11) The *Adjudicator* may, within two weeks of giving his decision to th Parties, correct any clerical mistake or ambiguity.

Review by the *tribunal* 94.4 (1) A Party does not refer any dispute under or in connection with thi contract to the *tribunal* unless it has first been referred to the *Adjudicator* i accordance with this contract.

(2) If, after the *Adjudicator* notifies his decision a Party is dissatisfied, he ma notify the other Party that he intends to refer it to the *tribunal*. A Party may nc refer a dispute to the *tribunal* unless this notification is given within fot weeks of notification of the *Adjudicator*'s decision.

(3) If the *Adjudicator* does not notify his decision within the time provided b this contract, a Party may notify the other Party that he intends to refer th dispute to the *tribunal*. A Party may not refer a dispute to the *tribunal* unles this notification is given within four weeks of the date by which the *Adjudicatc should have notified his decision.

(4) The *tribunal* settles the dispute referred to it. The *tribunal* has the power to reconsider any decision of the *Adjudicator* and review and revise any actio or inaction of the *Supply Manager* related to the dispute. A Party is not limite in the *tribunal* proceedings to the information, evidence or arguments put t the *Adjudicator*.

(5) If the *tribunal* is arbitration, the *arbitration procedure*, the place where th arbitration is to be held and the method of choosing the arbitrator are thos stated in the Contract Data.

(6) A Party does not call the *Adjudicator* as a witness in *tribunal* proceedings.

OPTION CLAUSES

Option X1: Price adjustment for inflation

Defined terms **X1**

X1.1 (a) The Base Date Index (B) is the latest available index before the *base date*.

(b) The Latest Index (L) is the latest available index before the assessment of an amount due.

(c) The Price Adjustment Factor is the total of the products of each of the proportions stated in the Contract Data multiplied by (L-B)/B for the index linked to it.

Price Adjustment Factor X1.2 If an index is changed after it has been used in calculating a Price Adjustment Factor, the calculation is repeated and a correction included in the next assessment of the amount due.

The Price Adjustment Factor calculated at the Delivery Date of the *goods* and *services* is used for calculating price adjustment after this date.

Compensation events X1.3 The change to the Prices for a compensation event is assessed using the change to the Prices current at the time of assessing the compensation event adjusted to *base date* by dividing by one plus the Price Adjustment Factor for the last assessment of the amount due.

Price adjustment X1.4 Each amount due includes an amount for price adjustment which is the sum of

- the change in

  - the Price for each lump sum item in the Price Schedule which the *Supplier* has completed and
  - where a quantity is stated for an item in the Price Schedule, the amount calculated by multiplying the quantity which the *Supplier* has completed by the rate,

  since the last assessment of the amount due multiplied by the Price Adjustment Factor for the date of the current assessment,

- the amount due for price adjustment included in the previous amount due and
- correcting amounts, not included elsewhere, which arise from changes to indices used for assessing previous amounts for price adjustment.

Option X2: Changes in the law

Changes in the law **X2**

X2.1 A change in the law of the country stated in the Contract Data is a compensation event if it occurs after the Contract Date. The *Supply Manager* may notify the *Supplier* of a compensation event for a change in the law and instruct him to submit quotations. If the effect of a compensation event which is a change in the law is to reduce the total Defined Cost, the Prices are reduced.

Option X3: Multiple currencies

Multiple currencies X3

X3.1   The *Supplier* is paid in currencies other than the *currency of this contract* for the items of *goods* and *services* listed in the Contract Data. The *exchange rates* are used to convert from the *currency of this contract* to other currencies.

X3.2   Payments to the *Supplier* in currencies other than the *currency of this contract* do not exceed the maximum amounts stated in the Contract Data. Any excess is paid in the *currency of this contract*.

Option X4: Parent company guarantee

**Parent company X4
guarantee**

X4.1   If a parent company owns the *Supplier*, the *Supplier* gives to the *Purchaser* a guarantee by the parent company of the *Supplier*'s performance in the form set out in the Goods Information. If the guarantee was not given by the Contract Date, it is given to the *Purchaser* within four weeks of the Contract Date.

Option X7: Delay damages

Delay damages X7

X7.1   The *Supplier* pays delay damages at the rate stated in the Contract Data from the Delivery Date for each day until the earlier of

• Delivery and
• the date on which the *Purchaser* starts to make use of the *goods* and *services*.

X7.2   If the Delivery Date is changed to a later date after delay damages have been paid, the *Purchaser* repays the overpayment of damages with interest. Interest is assessed from the date of payment to the date of repayment and the date of repayment is an assessment date.

X7.3   If the *Purchaser* uses a part of the *goods* and *services* before Delivery, the delay damages are reduced from the date on which the part is used. The *Supply Manager* assesses the benefit to the *Purchaser* of using the part of the *goods* and *services* as a proportion of the benefit to the *Purchaser* of using the whole of the *goods* and *services* not previously used. The delay damages are reduced in this proportion.

Option X12: Partnering

**Identified and defined X12
terms**

X12.1   (1) The Partners are those named in the Schedule of Partners. The *Client* is a Partner.

(2) An Own Contract is a contract between two Partners which includes this Option.

core clauses

option clauses

contract data

(3) The Core Group comprises the Partners listed in the Schedule of Core Group Members.

(4) Partnering Information is information which specifies how the Partners work together and is either in the documents which the Contract Data states it is in or in an instruction given in accordance with this contract.

(5) A Key Performance Indicator is an aspect of performance for which a target is stated in the Schedule of Partners.

Actions X12.2 (1) Each Partner works with the other Partners to achieve the *Client's objective* stated in the Contract Data and the objectives of every other Partner stated in the Schedule of Partners.

(2) Each Partner nominates a representative to act for it in dealings with other Partners.

(3) The Core Group acts and takes decisions on behalf of the Partners on those matters stated in the Partnering Information.

(4) The Partners select the members of the Core Group. The Core Group decides how they will work and decides the dates when each member joins and leaves the Core Group. The *Client's* representative leads the Core Group unless stated otherwise in the Partnering Information.

(5) The Core Group keeps the Schedule of Core Group Members and the Schedule of Partners up to date and issues copies of them to the Partners each time either is revised.

(6) This Option does not create a legal partnership between Partners who are not one of the Parties in this contract.

Working together X12.3 (1) The Partners work together as stated in the Partnering Information and in a spirit of mutual trust and co-operation.

(2) A Partner may ask another Partner to provide information that he needs to carry out the work in his Own Contract and the other Partner provides it.

(3) Each Partner gives an early warning to the other Partners when he becomes aware of any matter that could affect the achievement of another Partner's objectives stated in the Schedule of Partners.

(4) The Partners use common information systems as set out in the Partnering Information.

(5) A Partner implements a decision of the Core Group by issuing instructions in accordance with its Own Contracts.

(6) The Core Group may give an instruction to the Partners to change the Partnering Information. Each such change to the Partnering Information is a compensation event which may lead to reduced Prices.

(7) The Core Group prepares and maintains a timetable showing the proposed timing of the contributions of the Partners. The Core Group issues a copy of the timetable to the Partners each time it is revised. The *Supplier* changes his programme if it is necessary to do so in order to comply with the revised timetable. Each such change is a compensation event which may lead to reduced Prices.

(8) A Partner gives advice, information and opinion to the Core Group and to other Partners when asked to do so by the Core Group. This advice, information and opinion relates to work that another Partner is carrying out under its Own Contract and is given fully, openly and objectively. The Partners show contingency and risk allowances in information about costs, prices and timing for future work.

(9) A Partner notifies the Core Group before subcontracting any work.

core clauses

option clauses

contract data

| Incentives | X12.4 | (1) A Partner is paid the amount stated in the Schedule of Partners if the target stated for a Key Performance Indicator is improved upon or achieved. Payment of the amount is due when the target has been improved upon or achieved and is made as part of the amount due in the Partner's Own Contract. |

(2) The *Client* may add a Key Performance Indicator and associated payment to the Schedule of Partners but may not delete or reduce a payment stated in the Schedule of Partners.

Option X13: Performance bond

| Performance bond | **X13** | |
| | X13.1 | The *Supplier* gives the *Purchaser* a performance bond, provided by a bank or insurer which the *Supply Manager* has accepted, for the amount stated in the Contract Data and in the form set out in the Goods Information. A reason for not accepting the bank or insurer is that its commercial position is not strong enough to carry the bond. If the bond was not given by the Contract Date, it is given to the *Purchaser* within four weeks of the Contract Date. |

Option X14: Advanced payment to the *Supplier*

Advanced payment	**X14**	
	X14.1	The *Purchaser* makes an advanced payment to the *Supplier* of the amount stated in the Contract Data.
	X14.2	The advanced payment is made either within four weeks of the Contract Date or, if an advanced payment bond is required, within four weeks of the later of

- the Contract Date and
- the date when the *Purchaser* receives the advanced payment bond.

The advanced payment bond is issued by a bank or insurer which the *Supply Manager* has accepted. A reason for not accepting the proposed bank or insurer is that its commercial position is not strong enough to carry the bond. The bond is for the amount of the advanced payment which the *Supplier* has not repaid and is in the form set out in the Goods Information. Delay in making the advanced payment is a compensation event.

| | X14.3 | The advanced payment is repaid to the *Purchaser* by the *Supplier* in instalments of the amount stated in the Contract Data and at the intervals stated in the Contract Data. An instalment is included in each amount due assessed after the period stated in the Contract Data has passed until the advanced payment has been repaid. |

Option X17: Low performance damages

| Low performance damages | **X17** | |
| | X17.1 | If a Defect which remains uncorrected at its *defects date* and shows low performance with respect to a performance level stated in the Contract Data, the *Supplier* pays the amount of low performance damages stated in the Contract Data. |

Option X20: Key Performance Indicators (not used with Option X12)

Incentives **X20**

X20.1 A Key Performance indicator is an aspect of performance by the *Supplier* for which a target is stated in the Incentive Schedule. The Incentive Schedule is the *incentive schedule* unless later changed in accordance with this contract.

X20.2 From the *starting date* until the last *defects date*, the *Supplier* reports to the *Supply Manager* his performance against each of the Key Performance Indicators. Reports are provided at the intervals stated in the Contract Data and include the forecast final measurement against each indicator.

X20.3 If the *Supplier's* forecast final measurement against a Key Performance Indicator will not achieve the target stated in the Incentive Schedule, he submits to the *Supply Manager* his proposals for improving performance.

X20.4 The *Supplier* is paid the amount stated in the Incentive Schedule if the target stated for a Key Performance Indicator is improved upon or achieved. Payment of the amount is due when the target has been improved upon or achieved.

X20.5 The *Purchaser* may add a Key Performance Indicator and associated payment to the Incentive Schedule but may not delete or reduce a payment stated in the Incentive Schedule.

core clauses

option clauses

contract data

Option Y(UK)1: Project Bank Account

Definitions **Y(UK)1**

Y1.1 (1) Project Bank Account is the account established by the *Purchaser* and used to make payments to the *Supplier*.

(2) Trust Deed is an agreement in the form set out in the contract which contains provisions for administering the Project Bank Account.

(3) Joining Deed is an agreement in the form set out in the contract under which the *Supplier* joins the Trust Deed.

Payments Y1.2 The *Supplier* receives payment from the Project Bank Account of the amount due from the *Purchaser* as soon as practicable after the Project Bank Account receives payment.

Y1.3 A payment which is due from the *Supplier* to the *Purchaser* is not made through the Project Bank Account.

Effect of payment Y1.4 Payments made from the Project Bank Account are treated as payments from the *Purchaser* to the *Supplier* in accordance with this contract.

If the *Supplier* is identified as a Named Supplier in the Contract Data for the *Purchaser's* contract with his employer

Trust Deed Y1.5 The *Purchaser*, his employer and the *Supplier* sign the Trust Deed before the first assessment date in the contract between the *Purchaser* and his employer.

If the *Supplier* is added as a Named Supplier after the Contract Date in the *Purchaser's* contract with his employer

Trust Deed Y1.5 The *Purchaser*, his employer and the *Supplier* sign the Joining Deed before the first assessment date.

Termination 1.6 If the *Supply Manager* issues a termination certificate, no further payment is made into the Project Bank Account.

core clauses

option clauses

contract data

Trust Deed

This agreement is made between the *Employer,* the *Contractor* and the Named Suppliers.

Terms in this deed have the meanings given to them in the contract between .... and .... for .... (the *works*).

Background

The *Employer* and the *Contractor* have entered into a contract for the *works.*

The Named Suppliers have entered into contracts with the *Contractor* or a Sub-contractor in connection with the *works.*

The *Contractor* has established a Project Bank Account to make provision for payment to the *Contractor* and the Named Suppliers.

Agreement

The parties to this deed agree that

- sums due to the *Contractor* and Named Suppliers and set out in the Authorisation are held in trust in the Project Bank Account by the *Contractor* for distribution to the *Contractor* and Named Suppliers in accordance with the banking arrangements applicable to the Project Bank Account,
- further Named Suppliers may be added as parties to this deed with the agreement of the *Employer* and *Contractor.* The agreement of the *Employer* and *Contractor* is treated as agreement by the Named Suppliers who are parties to this deed,
- this deed is subject to the law of the contract for the *works,*
- the benefits under this deed may not be assigned.

Executed as a deed on ....

by

.... (*Employer*)

.... (*Contractor*)

....

....

....

....

(Named Suppliers)

core clauses

option clauses

contract data

Joining Deed

This agreement is made between the *Employer,* the *Contractor* and .... (the Additional Supplier).

Terms in this deed have the meanings given to them in the contract between .... and .... for .... (the *works*).

Background

The *Employer* and the *Contractor* have entered into a contract for the *works.*

The Named Suppliers have entered into contracts with the *Contractor* or a Sub-contractor in connection with the *works*.

The *Contractor* has established a Project Bank Account to make provision for payment to the *Contractor* and the Named Suppliers.

The *Employer,* the *Contractor* and the Named Suppliers have entered into a deed as set out in Annex 1 (the Trust Deed), and have agreed that the Additional Supplier may join that deed.

Agreement

The Parties to this deed agree that

- the Additional Supplier becomes a party to the Trust Deed from the date set out below,
- this deed is subject to the law of the contract for the *works,*
- the benefits under this deed may not be assigned.

Executed as a deed on ....

by

.... (*Employer*)

.... (*Contractor*)

.... (Additional Supplier)

Option Y(UK)3: The Contracts (Rights of Third Parties) Act 1999

Third party rights **Y(UK)3**

Y3.1   A person or organisation who is not one of the Parties may enforce a term of this contract under the Contracts (Rights of Third Parties) Act 1999 only if the term and the person or organisation are stated in the Contract Data.

Option Z: *Additional conditions of contract*

Additional conditions of **Z1**
contract Z1.1   The *additional conditions of contract* stated in the Contract Data are part of this contract.

core clauses

option clauses

contract data

       37

CONTRACT DATA

Part one – Data provided by the *Purchaser*

Completion of the data in full, according to the Options chosen, is essential to create a complete contract.

Statements given in all contracts

1 General

- The *conditions of contract* are the core clauses and the clauses for Options ...... of the NEC3 Supply Contract April 2013.
- The *goods* are

  ....

- The *services* are

  ....

- The *Purchaser* is

  Name ....

  Address ....

  ....

- The *Supply Manager* is

  Name ....

  Address ....

  ....

- The *Adjudicator* is

  Name ....

  Address ....

- The Goods Information is in

  ....

  ....

  ....

- The Supply Requirements as part of the Goods Information is in

  ....

  ....

- The *language of this contract* is ....
- The *law of the contract* is the law of ....
- The *period for reply* is .... weeks
- The *Adjudicator nominating body* is ....

- The *tribunal* is . . . .

- The following matters will be included in the Risk Register

  . . . .

  . . . .

  . . . .

  . . . .

  . . . .

3 Time

- The *starting date* is . . . .

- The *Supplier* submits revised programmes at intervals no longer than . . . . . . weeks.

4 Testing and Defects

- The *defects date* is . . . . weeks after Delivery.

- The *defect correction period* is . . . . weeks except that

  - The *defect correction period* for . . . . is . . . . weeks

  - The *defect correction period* for . . . . is . . . . weeks.

- The *defect access period* is . . . . days except that

  - The *defect access period* for . . . . is . . . .

  - The *defect access period* for . . . . is . . . .

5 Payment

- The *currency of this contract* is the . . . .

- The *assessment interval* is . . . . weeks (not more than five).

- The *interest rate* is . . . . % per annum (not less than 2) above the . . . . rate of the . . . . bank.

8 Risks, liabilities, indemnities and insurance

- The minimum limit of indemnity for insurance in respect of loss of or damage to property (except the *goods*, plant and materials and equipment) and liability for bodily injury to or death of a person (not an employee of the *Supplier*) caused by activity in connection with this contract for any one event is

  . . . .

- The minimum limit of indemnity for insurance in respect of death of or bodily injury to employees of the *Supplier* arising out of and in the course of their employment in connection with this contract for any one event is

  . . . .

- The *Supplier*'s liability to the *Purchaser* for indirect or consequential loss including loss of profit, revenue and goodwill is limited to . . . .

- For any one event, the *Supplier*'s liability to the *Purchaser* for loss of or damage to the *Purchaser*'s property is limited to . . . .

- The *Supplier*'s liability for Defects due to his design which are not notified before the last *defects date* is limited to . . . .

  The *Supplier*'s total liability to the *Purchaser* for all matters arising under or in connection with this contract, other than the excluded matters, is limited to . . . .

- The *end of liability date* is . . . . years after Delivery of the whole of the *goods* and *services*.

core clauses

option clauses

contract data

core
clauses

option
clauses

contract
data

Optional statements

If the *tribunal* is arbitration

- The *arbitration procedure* is . . . .
- The place where arbitration is to be held is

. . . .

- The person or organisation who will choose an arbitrator
  - if the Parties cannot agree a choice or
  - if the *arbitration procedure* does not state who selects an arbitrator is

. . . .

If the *Purchaser* is to state the *delivery date* of the *goods* and *services*

- The *delivery date* of the *goods* and *services* is

goods and services   delivery date

. . . .

. . . .

If no programme is identified in part two of the Contract Data

- The *Supplier* is to submit a first programme for acceptance within . . . . . .
weeks of the Contract Date.

If the *Supplier* is not to bring the *goods* to the Delivery Place more than one week before the Delivery Date

- The *Supplier* does not bring the *goods* to the Delivery Place more than one week before the Delivery Date.

If the period in which payments are made is not three weeks

- The period within which payments are made is . . . .

If there are additional *Purchaser*'s risks

- These are additional *Purchaser*'s risks
  1 . . . .
  2 . . . .
  3 . . . .

If the *Purchaser* is to provide any of the insurances stated in the Insurance Table

- The *Purchaser* provides these insurances from the Insurance Table

  1. Insurance against . . . .
  Cover/indemnity is . . . .
  The deductibles are . . . .
  2. Insurance against . . . .
  Cover/indemnity is . . . .
  The deductibles are . . . .

If additional insurances are to be provided

- The *Purchaser* provides these additional insurances

  1. Insurance against . . . .
  Cover/indemnity is . . . .
  The deductibles are . . . .

2. Insurance against . . . .

Cover/indemnity is . . . .

The deductibles are . . . .

- The *Supplier* provides these additional insurances

1. Insurance against . . . .

Cover/indemnity is . . . .

The deductibles are . . . .

2. Insurance against . . . .

Cover/indemnity is . . . .

The deductibles are . . . .

If Option X1 is used

- The proportions used to calculate the Price Adjustment Factor are

proportion	prepared by
0· . . . . linked to the index for	. . . .
0·	. . . .
0·	. . . .
0·	. . . .
0· . . . . non-adjustable	

1·00

- The *base date* for indices is . . . .

If Option X2 is used

- A change in the law of . . . . is a compensation event if it occurs after the Contract Date.

If Option X3 is used

- The *Purchaser* will pay for the items listed below in the currencies stated

items	other currency	total maximum payment in the currency
. . . .	. . . .	. . . .
. . . .	. . . .	. . . .
. . . .	. . . .	. . . .

- The *exchange rates* are those published in . . . .

on . . . . (date).

If Option X7 is used

- Delay damages for Delivery are

Delivery of	amount per day
. . . .	. . . .
. . . .	. . . .
. . . .	. . . .

core clauses

option clauses

contract data

If Option X12 is used

- The *Client* is

  Name . . . .

  Address . . . .

  . . . .

- The *Client*'s objective is . . . .
- The Partnering Information is in

  . . . .

If Option X13 is used

- The amount of the performance bond is . . . .

If Option X14 is used

- The amount of the advanced payment is . . . .
- The *Supplier* repays the instalments in assessments starting not less than

  . . . . weeks after the Contract Date

- The instalments are . . . .

  (either an amount or a percentage of the payment otherwise due)

- An advanced payment bond is/is not required.

If Option X17 is used

- The amounts for low performance damages are

  amount   performance level

  . . . .   for . . . .

  . . . .   for . . . .

  . . . .   for . . . .

  . . . .   for . . . .

If Option X20 is used (but not if Option X12 is also used)

- The *incentive schedule* for Key Performance Indicators is in

  . . . .

- A report of performance against each Key Performance Indicator is provided at intervals of . . . . months.

If Option Y(UK)1 is used and the *Purchaser* is to pay any charges made and is paid any interest paid by the *project bank*

- The *Purchaser* is to pay any charges made and is paid any interest paid by the *project bank*.

If Option Y(UK)3 is used

- term   person or organisation

  . . . .

  . . . .

  . . . .

  . . . .

core clauses

option clauses

contract data

If Options Y(UK)1 and Y(UK)3 are both used

- term   person or organisation

  The provisions of Option Y(UK)1   Named Suppliers

If Option Z is used

- The *additional conditions of contract* are . . . .

  . . . .

core
clauses

option
clauses

contract
data

Part two - Data provided by the *Supplier*

Completion of the data in full, according to the Options chosen, is essential to create a complete contract.

core
clauses

option
clauses

contract
data

**Statements given in
all contracts**

- The *Supplier* is

  Name . . . .

  Address . . . .

  . . . .

- The following matters will be included in the Risk Register

  . . . .

  . . . .

  . . . .

  . . . .

- The *percentage for overheads and profit* added to the Defined Cost is

  . . . . %

- The *price schedule* is in . . . .

- The tendered total of the Prices is . . . . (in words)

  . . . .

Optional statements

If the *Supplier* is to provide Goods Information for his design

- The Goods Information for the *Supplier*'s design is in

  . . . .

  . . . .

If the *Supplier* restricts access by the *Supply Manager* and Others to work being done for this contract

- The restrictions to access for the *Supply Manager* and Others to work being done for this contract are

  . . . .

  . . . .

If a programme is to be identified in the Contract Data

- The programme identified in the Contract Data is . . . .

If the *Supplier* is to state the *delivery date* of the *goods* and *services*

- The *delivery date* of the *goods* and *services* is

  goods and *services*   *delivery date*

  . . . .

If Option Y(UK)1 is used

- The *project bank* is . . . .

- *named suppliers* are . . . .

Index by clause numbers (Option clauses indicated by their letters, main clause heads by bold numbers). Terms in *italics* are identified in Contract Data, and defined terms have capital initial letters.